SOFT ARRIVALS

SOFT ARRIVALS

Audrey Tanner

Kinstu Books

Soft Arrivals
Copyright © 2024 by Audrey Tanner

Revised Edition 2026

Published by Kinstu Books in the USA

Cover design by Audrey Tanner using elements from Canva.com. Elements attributions: @Backyard Productions via Canva.com; @ksuview via Canva.com; @Alex8429 via Canva.com.

Ebook ISBN: 979-8-9896979-3-9
Paperback ISBN: 979-8-9896979-4-6

For Valentim.
For soft closures, and even softer openings.

Introduction

Soft Arrivals is poetry inspired by the author's first visit to the beautiful island of Madeira, Portugal.

A stop at the Museum of Ethnography (Museu Etnográfico da Madeira) in Riveira Brava influenced imagery in this poetry as equally as Madeira's natural beauty and sense of being on the island.

While every place on the island inspires poetry, this book mentions only a few places. More poetry about Madeira is anticipated, along with more visits to the island.

May you, the reader, find something meaningful within.

Contents

ARRIVALS 1

THE SWEETEST KISS 11

THEN YOU MAY SWIM 19

FUNCHAL, EARLY MORNING 29

SKY LIKE BLANCHED PLUMS 43

SHADOWS AND RITUALS 51

POETRY OF CLOUDS 59

CURES OF AN ISLAND 65

INTO OCEAN 75

FISHERMEN 81

BIRDS TELLING STORIES 87

CLOUDS COMING INTO SKY 95

PONTA DO PARGO, MIST 105

SUNRISE, FUNCHAL 113

CLOSING CIRCLES 119

ARRIVALS

You hope
for an island
only when
you are
surrounded
by sky and sea;

only then
can you step
onto land,
can you dust
into daylight
all your being.

Touching down
in an
airplane,
it is only after
you debark

that you notice
the sound
of the island
softly calling
you into
yourself.

Breathing in
the sense
of being
in island
flower scent;

only then
can you see
how island bloom
opens
the subdued
parts of the self.

Where the bay
near Funchal
forms a half
moon-shaped
embrace,

then can you
notice
how you
emerge from
your wildness
into softness?

Into soft air
you follow
road signs
leading to
sharp mountain
valleys;

only then
do you see
how Funchal
is a soft town
where you
can melt
into being.

Into mountains
above Funchal
you carry
yourself
as an old man
is carried;

only then can you
fly as a hawk
flies, wheeling
fresh air
over pathways
of self.

You slip onto
switchbacks
as if
slipping
with rock fall;

only then
do you see
tunnels,
how to pass
through darkness
to light
being of self.

THE SWEETEST KISS

I wait because you wait
while the sun
lights the surface
of an ocean,
while an ocean comes ashore.

In this there is
the sweetest kiss;

the sun reaches
mouth to mouth,
sunrays and water.

Here the ocean is
an old woman
with soft skin
telling her stories.

I wait because you wait
while the sun dances
into late afternoon,

while the ocean becomes
grace of pen and fingers,
an old woman's shadows,
the writing of poems.

This is how a sun sets:
still, with the sea still coming.

This is how the sun
slants rays into knowing.

I move with soft movements
because the sea moves.

I move into you
as a soft wave of water,
waiting as you wait
until evening
brings up the soft stir
of sea scent and rose bloom.

I look because you look
into diffractions of waves,
an ocean of stories;

how sun sinks,
how clouds become
sea and sky sameness.

I glimpse because you glimpse
how into nothingness
mountains dissipate,
into soft shadows,
hulking darknesses
of self, poetry.

I look until I become blind
as you fuse into sunset,
into ocean and sky.

I wait because you wait
knowing of sunrise,
how light slants over mountains,

how this will become
another kiss;
mouth to mouth,
sun and water,
brilliance.

THEN YOU MAY SWIM

Here, the ocean is
soft, with an
old woman's skin,
and as full
of her stories.

She is grandmother
opening her arms
to gather up
familial waves,
brothers and cousins,
mantas and grouper.

Time is her mystery;
she has become
old and soft
if only to show you
how to swim into her.

She invites you
to plunge
beneath waves
to feel the sum
of all that she is,
sisters and mothers,
dolphins and whales.

Show her how
your body floats,
how you dive
into her to receive
a water blessing,
a soft baptism.

As a grandchild
she will receive you;
she will wash
your face,
your hands.

She will take you
into her kitchen
of ocean
teeming with scents
seaweed and salt,
the magic
of her ingredients.

You may only
swim, but don't you feel
how she kneads you
body to body
with the hands
of a strong woman?

Kneading you into
soft bread,
she will roll you
onto a shore she has
worn down
to lava crag,
stone and cliff wall.

Onto an island
self, she will roll
you – then
let her roll you
from the shore
into her soft folds
and depth.

You may float in her
feeling as if you
were fish;
you may
weave through waves
as you swim.

Here, the ocean is
warp and weft,
threads pushed
into place
into oceany
cloth, a mantle,
subtle embroidery.
This from a woman
thick from a hard life.

In waves her voice
calls dolphins;
with currents
she shows you how
she weaves them into
fibers of linen
and spun wool.

Let her weave you
into her skirt
to wrap you
as an island is wrapped:
crochet surf,
lace froth of water.

She will spin you
into the threads
of watery cloth
coming shoreward,
diffuse as
the knitted pattern
of a soft skirt
dyed in the colors
of sunrise and sunset.

Then you may swim
into the colors of her,
sweet hues of water
and dancing sun.

FUNCHAL, EARLY MORNING

Sunrise, you look east
because
with the color of water
there is silver slipping
between tones
of gray, green, blue.

Here the ocean is
always
shifting to slip
between ripples, fractions
of a fraction, multiple
surfaces, all adding up
to wholeness.

You are like that too
sometimes,
moment by moment
a sea of change.

While the city awakes
with movement,
you can stand still
in the steady hum
of busses, cars;
you can be the one
who is chanting
the sound of waves,
the lull of ocean.

Here, you can remember
an ocean
for the way
she pauses. She offers
you a chance
to catch sunlight
sparkle on her surface.

Near shore, the water
seems green-gold
and calm, sheltered
by the arms of pier.
It is only when you
move into her,
when you
are miles out,
that you notice
how the water is
pure and blue.

You can swim in this sea
with care;
you can dip into her with
grace, stepping from a ladder
or diving from
the side of a boat
to look towards
the curl of island.

When you swim, you
attune to soft patterns
of self;
this is how the sunrise
glances, slanting
light until
you are illuminated
and full.

Here in the cloudless morning
you become
as the sea:
soft
as an embroidered blanket
taking shape into
the curve of bay.

Light shapes
nuances of mountains
and gorges,
a city unwrapping
the quilt of itself
towards sea.

You are here in this sunrise.
You are mountain
and ocean, city illuming
into day, a moment
fog lifting,
haze light, sun glow.

SKY LIKE BLANCHED PLUMS

Funchal, here you merge
into sky the color
of blanched plums;

sky hiding angels and stars;
the moon somewhere
above a quilt of fog.

You become mysterious
and sensuous,
tucked into refractions,
soft mauve.

Waking into sky
that is the color
of indefiniteness,

you become a dance
of street light and night,
the color of sepia-plum,

cloud cover
as if raisin wash
tucked into night,
a soft dream.

Funchal, you give
a night sky that is
clouded and folded

as intricate as
delicate whale bone,
a hand-held fan
of floral silk.

Women hold you,
waving shades of dusk rose
and midnight.

You are full
brimming with clouds
and ocean scent;

into midnight you sweep
soft dreams
for men who will wake
to woo you with

bouquets
of statice
the color
of orchid haze.

Beneath clouds
you dance into fog;
your mountaintops
dissipate.

Into night
you become a dream
of arrival,

angels touching
wings of faded violet
to dust you
into day.

SHADOWS AND RITUALS

Here is a room
full of her shadows.
Into this, open
cloister doors,
air out cloth.

Here is a ritual
of women
to clear the soul.

Here is a folk story,
water and herbs.

All this is holy;
all this is ritual.

Take mantles and lace,
take mattress and chair;
sweep from the floor
all the shadowy dust.

Take into a glass
oil and water;
into cloth over her head,
a chant to the virgin.

Here is a room
that must be cleansed
of its shadows;
she has been born
for a miracle.

Here is how she
threshed flax until
she could be
brushed like hair
of a young girl.

Here is a loom,
a basket of thread
dyed in the hues
of mothers and newborns.
Here is knowing.

Take into hands
strands of linen;
how she weaves them
into delicate patterns.

Here is cloth and shroud,
shadow and thread
as holy as air,
as intricate
as breathing.

Into a church
she may stumble;
there she is a temple
of self, all wood beam
and gilt,
substance and shadow.

Here is a ritual
of incense and candle;
here is an offering,
a soul for a soul.

POETRY OF CLOUDS

Poetry of clouds
always
shaped like islands,
communities,
rivers and families,
sisters and sons;
always
spill of cloud over sky
into
longing,
a hand held,
a dance,
a prayer,
soft angels.

Spill of cloud along
horizon,
always
drift;
always
cloud-drift with sea
into
sea-cloud drift,
into
cloud like butterfly flit,
into
morph and flow,
dream diffusion,
winged angels.

On a cold mountain
always
unfold and fall
into
all the same color;
into
cloud mist breathing,
water and life,
into
cloud being
breath and wind,
always
cloud mind opening,
form of angels.

CURES OF AN ISLAND

Toe-dip, then
foot, ankle,
then immersion
up to knees
until it becomes
clear in
the black sand
on the rock beach
how the body
wants
to fully feel
roll of ocean,
self,
excursion:

a cure
of water,

a washing out
of soul.

At the rock beach
you sit, you take
a soft stone
and hope
it has within it
curl of oceans past;
a fossil, meaning
ammonite,
connection, eons:

a cure
so fundamental

it is solidified
into stone

yet still of
your soul.

Sunburn
in the bright
afternoon, bare
hint
of shadow;
you muse
how close
you must be
to the Sahara,
a connection
to past self,
an ancestor:

double-helixed
and embodied,

DNA,
a long cure.

So many cures
in the purse
of the ocean:
open your
senses
to find cures
of salt breeze
and heart melt
in warm sun,
light dancing
on the fractal
surfaces of waves,
whitecaps
as breeze picks
up, as afternoon

and soul
deepens.

Open your heart
to a cure
of sea sound:
wash of surf,
waves cresting,
movement
of circadian
water, flow
of vein sound
into ocean,
heartbeat
synchronous;

here is a rush
of soul

matching rhythms
of sea.

Hum of boats
crossing water
is a cure:
a motor
not silenced;
in this at night
there is the cure
of a ship
lit up, casting
light as if
it is a small sun;
into this you pour
your soul

until suns
disappear

into deep
quiet, night water.

Night rise
and stars
deep into the dome
of sky;
along the horizon
are small suns
distant as if
lanterns;

you awake
into this
at 3 am
to pour

the milky way
into your soul:

a cure
of all cures.

INTO OCEAN

There is nothing but ocean.
Into this you may cast a net;

in a net catching
scent of ocean,
drift of wave.

Cast yourself and currents
will take you until
through palms of hands
you let water run.

You move into vastness
until you are sea;

cast from a net of self
you are no one.

Adrift as you are
you may spill
into water lacing
as dolphins lace.

The sea becomes
expanse and expanding:

this is how
you become wind-shorn;
you become whitecap
and swell.

Lacing fingers together, water runs
until you are cleansed.

FISHERMEN

Here in the gold-blue,

in the brown-green sea,
in the bay near shore,

here is the woman
of the sea,
old like a wood boat
barnacled and hauled ashore,

hull like a bosom
warmed in the sun.

Hear her lulling waves,
how she calls
the wild souls of fishermen.

They arrive
with palms open
with hook-scarred hands;

into boats of painted wood
they arrive in wide hats

and with hearts
full of hope.

From the mountains
they tumble, men full
of fish dreams;

into the sea they tumble.
She washes them
as if newborns.

Into this baptism of ocean
they come, bringing
their carved hooks
and woven nets.

She shows them
where to cast their hooks.

These mighty fishermen,
from boats of their souls,
they cast their nets.

She will give them
black scabbardfish and bream;

from her watery bosom
she gives
a rejoice of the sea.

BIRDS TELLING STORIES

Out of the city
into mountain
and the sea,
birds
tell their stories

in the cool
morning
before
the sun,

before people
rise and go
to terraced fields,

before people stir
into their coffee
the sound
of owls
recounting
the night's hunt.

You may circle
as a hawk
with gold-brown
wings, over
a hillside,
a mountain tumble,

over bare trees
with black trunks
that tell stories
of fire, how a hill
can become
creosote-stained
as much as a hearth.

You may fly
as a wren flies
into a careful ruin

of thick stone
fashioned in the shape
of a farmer's stories;
here, a wren

may scratch
amid weeds and shards

into the loam
of ancestor's being
on an old hearth
in the cool morning.

Here birds lay
their burnt feet
onto branches
until they can again
string nests
of grass and twigs;

here, as
new leaves grow,

birds return
to watch
how you fly
over ghosts
of infernos past,
over tree blight
and old things.

Here is a light bellied
swallow's song.
This is what she sings;

how she watches
people dreaming
all the shards
of their stories,

how the sun always
rises, sky shifts
into its blueness

while a silver-white
shadow of moon hangs
until church bells ring
into morning.

CLOUDS COMING INTO SKY

Moon, she still hangs
half an orb, high,
all silver-white;

clouds in wind
in an atmosphere
move past her,
touching mist
to moon's mouth.

Clouds come waking
a sky still asleep
with mystery
of what they may bring.

Ocean breeze moves clouds
inward to awaken,
in cool dawn,
hint and promise of day.

Sky may have been dreaming,
sunrise not yet
becoming;

clouds move into
swathing
of mountains
hues of gray cotton.

Clouds come into sky
as if dream;
mountains sleep
in the still morning,

in quiet dawn
while over an ocean
breeze gathers,
moon hangs;
complete surrender,
her cloudy kiss.

Sunrise in clouds brings
gray into hues
flora greens, earth reds;

oceans of scent
heady and sweet
in a rose-tail,
among grape wisp
and weed.

Cloud shadow shows
yellow lily poking
her head like a sun.

Cloud in breeze moving
bird trill and silence,
fennel froth of flower
and scent of sea,
lemon and spruce.

Sea caps
appear spume white,
stirring with morning

while clouds in
palm frond breeze
and grape vine dancing
move into day,
sun dance and shadow.

PONTA DO PARGO, MIST

All you can hear is wind,
wind that pushes clouds,
clouds that tumble
down mountains
as fog and mist;
clouds cover the sea.

Everything becomes diffuse,
all the same nature,
the sea the color
of silver-blue,
the sea the color
of mist on a mountain.

Everywhere the sea moves,
clouds move
water to water,
vapor to vapor,
until you are shivering
as if you are mist.

Here is a mystery to enter
just by walking
garden to garden,
mist thick as rain,
finding as you find
rose and grape glisten.

Move as you move
through mountain mist;
ocean swirls into you,
mountain crests spiral
into your lungs
as watery breath.

Take this into your being
as shapeless haze,
drizzle of cloud,
a touch of sea,
soft water beading
into your soul.

SUNRISE, FUNCHAL

Step out of night
into daylight, into the way
shadow becomes light.

Here is a way
light sweeps over mountains
becoming self, soul.

Here is a way the sun rises,
pushing through boundaries,
revealing there are none.

Walk down a city street
until you reach
a bay, water, a place

where light refracts
gentle movement, revealing
in waves, only light.

Here is a way sun shows you
how to pause into self,
to let go of reflections.

Into sunrise you can promise
to let go your shadows,
to let sunlight wash you.

Water and mountains release
nuances of the soul
in sunlight's touch.

Here is a way the sun greets you:
first a glimpse, then slanting
until it is fullness.

CLOSING CIRCLES

Packing suitcase while
the island sings to you;

breeze through pine
and sugar cane,
palm trees and bird
of paradise;

all these melodies
closing.

Island singing its goodbye
with wind picked up
with waves of white caps,

while mountains
form circles around you,
bow down to touch water,
close into you knowing
a closure is opening.

You will cross oceans
trying to remember
how the sea is
singing its blue
goodbye,

how waves roll
in circles
open and closing,

shifting soft melodies
of waves and surf.

Here is an intricate song:

diamonds sparkling
in the crests of whitecaps,
symphony
of islands
and small boats
bobbing in the waves
like dolphins
weaving ocean

as if it were linen clothing
laid out for your journey.

You will have an airplane
lifting you into sky;
you will have a window
overlooking sea.

There will be
tension of leaving
in the lyric of wind,

vibration like guitar strings
beneath calloused fingers,
circles closing.

In the air
a trace of eucalyptus
and wild flower bloom,
salt of the sea;

a swallow sings its
bird trill,

a hint of what
will wait for you,

a gentle return,
new circles opening.

ABOUT THE AUTHOR

Audrey Tanner, Ed.D., is a poet and healer dedicated to the art of self-restoration. As a Reiki Master in the Usui lineage and a certified teacher of yoga and meditation, her writing is an extension of her spiritual practice—a bridge between the physical landscape and the inner soul.

With a doctorate in higher education leadership and over 30 years of university experience, Audrey blends a grounded, scholarly perspective with a deep mastery of Sanskrit mantra and mindfulness. A graduate of the UCLA Extension fiction writing program, she now explores the "quiet magic" of the world through poetry and creative nonfiction. *Soft Arrivals* is her invitation to readers to slow down, breathe, and find their way home to themselves.

audreytannerwrites.com

MORE BY AUDREY TANNER

SLOW MOVING CLOUDS: Poems from Madeira Island that invite the reader into a peaceful experience of awarenesses, imagination, and self-renewal within an atmospheric quietness born of the island's natural beauty.

RIVER DREAM: Peaceful poems for meditation, self-reflection, daydreaming, and dreams. Nature as a presence that guides the journey into the depth of self.

KARMAS, LIKE HEARTS: A poetry chapbook. Poems about an experience of loss, grief, and recovery that guide the reader with grace from loss to light.

YOU ARE ALWAYS CIRCLING: Meditative poems exploring how the same daily walk reveals connections between nature and self, allowing for peace, self-forgiveness, and revealing what is hidden in the quest to return to innermost self and heart-centered being.

www.ingramcontent.com/pod-product-compliance
Lightning Source LLC
Chambersburg PA
CBHW020402130626
46549CB00006B/2399